Kay Gardiner and Ann Shayne

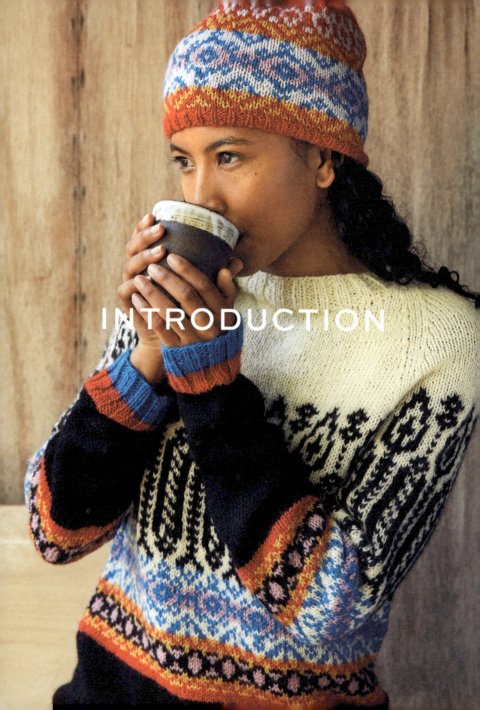

INTRODUCTION

W E'RE OFF TO NORWAY, with the best possible guides: Arne and Carlos. The Norwegian tourist board should thank its lucky stars for these two—they are endlessly entertaining when talking about their homeland, and their love of Norway's traditional handknitting is wildly infectious.

Arne Nerjordet and Carlos Zachrisson are renowned as fashion designers, textile artists, and authors. They travel the world to share their enthusiasm. And their weekly podcast on YouTube, *Sit and Knit for a Bit*, is good addicting fun, with never-ending discussion about knitting, crochet, and life in the Norwegian countryside.

A conversation with Arne and Carlos might go like this: you start talking about a hat pattern, and before you know it, you've heard about the latest Prada collection, 12th-century Norwegian knitting lore, and why Italian mills are the best. Plus the extreme importance of cinnamon rolls and coffee.

In this Field Guide, Arne and Carlos's deep understanding of Norway's traditional textiles as well as their passion for color are on full display—and it's all combined with their sophisticated design sense.

Here we enter a world where a standard sweater style gets a makeover, where embroidery motifs become knitting motifs, where traditional colorways meet millennial pink.

The Valdres Pullover is a wintertime stunner—a project to treasure forever—named after the region where Arne and Carlos live, which happens to be one of the snowiest places in the country.

The Kos Neckwarmer is pure whimsy (and a fantastic layer when the winds blow), chock full of hearts, diamonds, and zigzags.

The Setesdal Hat, like the Valdres Pullover, is a canvas for playing with colorwork motifs. And the stranded fabric keeps the chill out.

Rosy Mittens are traditional in silhouette and technique, knitted in two high-contrast colors, with sparks of embellishment added while you go or in duplicate stitch once the knitting is complete.

There is something about Arne and Carlos that encourages us to snuggle up, draw close to the fireplace, and light a candle. They make us want to visit their world—and make what they're making. Their invitation is simple: please join the fun.

Kay   Ann

STRANDED KNITTING 101

All of the projects in this Field Guide call for stranded knitting, a technique that requires us to change colors every stitch or every few stitches within a round. To do this, we need to know how to hold the yarns so that they don't tangle. The following method, holding one color in each hand, is our favorite.

1. Hold the needles loosely in your hands. Drape Color A across the top of your right index finger, front to back.

    Drape Color B across the top of your left index finger, front to back. Your thumbs and other fingers hold the needles in place.

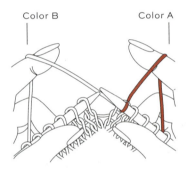

1.

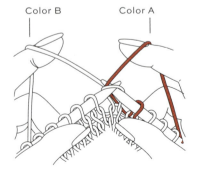

2.

2. To knit Color A, insert the right needle knitwise into the next stitch.

    Using your right index finger, knit Color A.

Color B   Color A

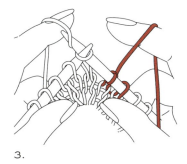

3.

The stitches made with the yarn in your left hand will be ever so slightly larger than the stitches made with the yarn in your right hand. To make your pattern stand out, work the pattern yarn with your left hand, and the background yarn with your right hand.

3. To knit Color B, insert the right needle knitwise into the next stitch.

As you work, you will see horizontal strands of yarn across the back of your fabric. These strands need a bit of slack. To create that slack, when you change to a new color of yarn, slightly spread apart the stitches on your right needle as you bring the new color behind them.

Using your left index finger, pull Color B so that it is somewhat snug—not too loose or too tight.

Move the tip of the right needle to the right of Color B, then move it behind Color B.

Color B is now over the right needle, going from front to back. With the right needle, pull Color B through to complete a knit stitch.

Yarn stranded at back of work

SETESDAL HAT

Design by
Arne & Carlos

THE POTENTIAL FOR color experimentation on this quick knit is excellent—going light or dark for the main color will change the effect completely. The motifs here originated in the Setesdal Valley in southern Norway. With a little math, you can switch out one or two of them with the motifs on the Valdres Pullover or Kos Neckwarmer. All three projects are worked in the same yarn at the same gauge, so mix and match to your heart's content—just keep an eye on your row count.

KNITTED MEASUREMENTS

Approx 20.25" (51.5 cm) circumference
along lower edge x 10" (25.5 cm) length

MATERIALS

- Norwegian Wool by Arne & Carlos
  for Rowan [50 g skeins, each approx
  137 yds (125 m), 100% wool]: 1 ball
  each #018 Ribbon Red (A), #012
  Gold Nugget (B), #010 Wind Chime
  (C), #011 Daphne (D), and #020
  Frost Pink (E)
- Size US 2 (3 mm) circular needle, 16"
  (40 cm) long
- Size US 4 (3.5 mm) circular needle,
  16" (40 cm) long, and double-
  pointed needles (set of 4 or 5), or
  size needed to achieve gauge
- Stitch marker

GAUGE

22 sts and 28 rnds = 4" (10 cm) over
stranded st st, using larger needle,
blocked

STITCH PATTERN

1×2 Rib

All Rnds: *K1, p2; rep from * to end.

Hat Chart

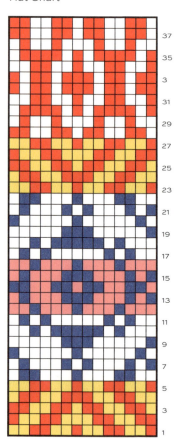

Color Key

- A
- B
- C
- D
- E

HAT

- Using smaller needle and A, CO 111 sts. Join, being careful not to twist sts; pm for beg of rnd and work in the rnd as follows:
- Beg 1×2 Rib; work 6 rnds even.
- Change to larger needle.
- Knit 1 rnd, inc 1 st at end of rnd—112 sts.
- Beg Hat Chart; work Rnds 1–38 of chart. Cut B, C, D, and E; continue in A for remainder of piece.
- Knit 1 rnd.

SHAPE CROWN

Note: Change to dpns when necessary for number of sts on needle.

- *Set-Up Rnd:* *K28, pm; rep from * to end, omitting last pm (beginning-of-rnd marker is here).
- *Dec Rnd:* *Ssk, knit to 2 sts before marker, k2tog; rep from * to end—8 sts dec.
- Rep Dec Rnd every other rnd 11 more times—16 sts rem.
- Knit 1 rnd.
- Cut yarn, leaving a 4" (10 cm) tail. Thread tail through rem sts, pull tight and fasten off.
- Weave in ends. Block as desired.

COLORWORK CHART TIPS

Part of the fun with stranded knitting is getting the hang of your chart. Here are some tips for success.

Look for symmetry. Many colorwork charts are symmetrical, which means that the second half of a pattern is the same as the first, only reversed.

Look for landmarks in the pattern. Some elements are likely to continue for a number of rounds, which helps you orient yourself in the pattern, for example, a vertical stack of stitches, or a stretch of one color.

Once you've completed a full repeat of the pattern, you can ditch your chart and refer to the rounds below instead. Pretty soon you may realize you have memorized the pattern without even trying.

VALDRES PULLOVER

Design by
Arne & Carlos

IF YOU'RE ON THE LOOKOUT for your first Scandinavian sweater project, we humbly point you toward this winning design, which combines traditional motifs with a modern palette of colors.

It's all worked in the round, with some easy stretches of stockinette before and after the more demanding stranded knitting. The sleeves come first, then the body, working from the hem upward. Once the sleeves and body are joined, the yoke is worked up to the neckline. Grafting under the arms is the only finishing required.

Absolutely gorgeous, worked here in Rowan Norwegian Wool, the yarn that Arne and Carlos designed with wool from Norwegian sheep, a hardy lot to be sure.

KNITTED MEASUREMENTS

Bust: 35 (39.25, 43.75, 48, 52.25) (56.75, 61, 65.5, 69.75)" [89 (99.5, 111, 122, 132.5) (144, 155, 166.5, 177) cm]

Length: 24 (24.5, 24.75, 25, 25.25) (25.5, 26, 26.5, 27)" [61 (62, 63, 63.5, 64) (65, 66, 67.5, 68.5) cm]

SIZES

To fit bust sizes 30-32 (34-36, 38-40, 42-44, 46-48) (50-52, 54-56, 58-60, 62-64)" [76-81.5 (86.5-91.5, 96.5-101.5, 106.5-112, 117-122) (127-132, 137-142, 147.5-152.5, 157.5-162.5) cm]

MATERIALS

— Rowan Norwegian Wool [50 g skeins, each 137 yds (125 m), 100% wool]: 2 (2, 2, 2, 2) (2, 2, 2, 3) balls #011 Daphne (A); 1 (1, 2, 2, 2) (2, 2, 2, 2) ball(s) #018 Ribbon Red (B); 3 (3, 4, 4, 4) (5, 5, 5, 6) balls #019 Peat (C); 1 (1, 1, 1, 1) (1, 1, 2, 2) ball(s) #012 Gold Nugget (D); 1 ball #020 Frost Pink (E); 4 (4, 4, 5, 5) (5, 6, 6, 6) balls #021 Vanilla Custard (F)

— Size US 2 (3 mm) circular needles, 16" and 32" (40 and 80 cm) long, and double-pointed needles (set of 4 or 5)

— Size US 4 (3.5 mm) circular needles, 16", 24", and 32" (40, 60, and 80 cm) long, and double-pointed needles (set of 4 or 5), or size needed to achieve gauge

— Stitch markers

GAUGES

22 sts and 28 rnds = 4" (10 cm) over st st, using larger needle, blocked

22 sts and 28 rnds = 4" (10 cm) over stranded st st, using larger needle, blocked

Note: you may need to go up a needle size when working stranded st st.

STITCH PATTERN

2×2 Rib

All Rnds: K1, p2, *k2, p2; rep from * to last st, k1.

NOTES

Sleeves are worked in round to underarm, then placed on hold while body is worked in round to underarm. Pieces are joined and yoke is worked in one piece to end, with raglan shaping. Sweater sizing is unisex, which is longer than women's sizing. Measure a favorite sweater, and adjust body length if necessary before beginning to work chart.

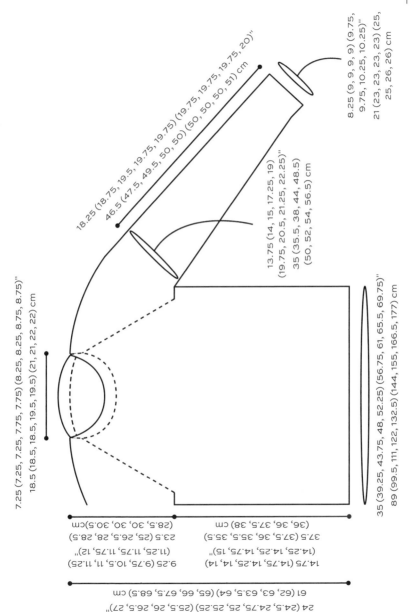

8.25 (9, 9, 9) (9.75, 9.75, 10.25, 10.25)"
21 (23, 23, 23) (25, 25, 26, 26) cm

18.25 (18.75, 19.5, 19.75, 19.75) (19.75, 19.75, 19.75, 20)"
46.5 (47.5, 49.5, 50, 50) (50, 50, 50, 51) cm

13.75 (14, 15, 17.25, 19) (19.75, 20.5, 21.25, 22.25)"
35 (35.5, 38, 44, 48.5) (50, 52, 54, 56.5) cm

35 (39.25, 43.75, 48, 52.25) (56.75, 61, 65.5, 69.75)"
89 (99.5, 111, 122, 132.5) (144, 155, 166.5, 177) cm

7.25 (7.25, 7.25, 7.75, 7.75) (8.25, 8.25, 8.75, 8.75)"
18.5 (18.5, 18.5, 19.5, 19.5) (21, 21, 22, 22) cm

9.25 (9.75, 10.5, 11, 11.25) (11.25, 11.75, 11.75, 12)"
23.5 (25, 26.5, 28, 28.5) (28.5, 30, 30, 30.5) cm

14.75 (14.75, 14.25, 14, 14) (14.25, 14.25, 14.75, 15)"
37.5 (37.5, 36, 35.5, 35.5) (36, 36, 37.5, 38) cm

24 (24.5, 24.75, 25, 25.25) (25.5, 26, 26.5, 27)"
61 (62, 63, 63.5, 64) (65, 66, 67.5, 68.5) cm

Sweater Chart Rounds 1–32

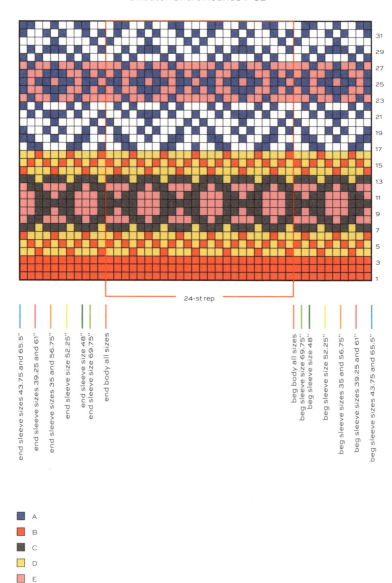

24-st rep

end sleeve sizes 43.75 and 65.5"
end sleeve sizes 39.25 and 61"
end sleeve sizes 35 and 56.75"
end sleeve size 52.25"
end sleeve size 48"
end sleeve size 69.75"
end body all sizes

beg body all sizes
beg sleeve size 69.75"
beg sleeve size 48"
beg sleeve size 52.25"
beg sleeve sizes 35 and 56.75"
beg sleeve sizes 39.25 and 61"
beg sleeve sizes 43.75 and 65.5"

- A
- B
- C
- D
- E
- F

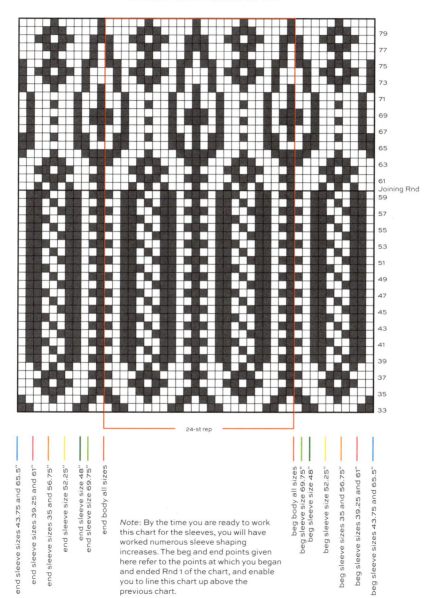

Note: By the time you are ready to work this chart for the sleeves, you will have worked numerous sleeve shaping increases. The beg and end points given here refer to the points at which you began and ended Rnd 1 of the chart, and enable you to line this chart up above the previous chart.

SLEEVES

— Using smaller dpns and A, CO 44 (48, 48, 48, 48) (52, 52, 56, 56) sts. Join, being careful not to twist sts; pm for beg of rnd and work in the rnd as follows:

— Begin 2×2 Rib; work 8 rnds.

— Change to B; work 8 more rnds in 2×2 Rib. Cut A and B.

— Change to larger dpns and C; knit 7 (6, 2, 7, 2) (2, 6, 6, 6) rnds, inc 1 st at beg of first rnd—45 (49, 49, 49, 49) (53, 53, 57, 57) sts.

SHAPE SLEEVE

— *Inc Rnd:* K1, M1R, work to last st, M1L, k1—2 sts inc.

— Continuing in st st, rep Inc Rnd every 6 (6, 6, 4, 2) (2, 2, 2, 2) rnds 7 (5, 9, 13, 1) (1, 7, 7, 12) more time(s), then every 0 (8, 0, 0, 4) (4, 4, 4, 4) rnds 0 (2, 0, 0, 14) (14, 10, 10, 8) time(s)—61 (65, 69, 77, 81) (85, 89, 93, 99) sts.

— Work even if necessary until piece measures 10 (10.5, 11.25, 11.5, 11.5) (11.5, 11.5, 11.5, 11.75)" [25.5 (26.5, 28.5, 29, 29) (29, 29, 29, 30) cm].

BEG CHART

Work Rnds 1–4 of Sweater Chart, beg and end where indicated for your size.

CONTINUE SLEEVE SHAPING

— Rep Inc Rnd on next rnd, then every 6 (8, 6, 4, 4) (4, 4, 4, 4) rnds 3 (5, 2, 2, 11) (11, 11, 11, 11) more time(s), then every 8 (0, 8, 6, 0) (0, 0, 0, 0) rnds 3 (0, 4, 6, 0) (0, 0, 0, 0) time(s)—75 (77, 83, 95, 105) (109, 113, 117, 123) sts.

— Work even through Rnd 59 of Chart. Cut yarn; place last 5 (6, 7, 8, 9) (11, 13, 15, 16) sts worked and first 5 (6, 7, 8, 9) (11, 13, 15, 16) sts of next rnd on one st holder for underarm (removing marker)—10 (12, 14, 16, 18) (22, 26, 30, 32) sts on holder. Place rem 65 (65, 69, 79, 87) (87, 87, 87, 91) sts on separate st holder or waste yarn and set aside.

BODY

— Using smaller 32" circular needle and A, CO 192 (216, 240, 264, 288) (312, 336, 360, 384) sts. Join, being careful not to twist sts; pm for beg of rnd and work in the rnd as follows:

— Begin 2×2 Rib; work 8 rnds.

— Change to B; work 8 more rnds in 2×2 Rib. Cut A and B.

— Change to larger needle and C; work in st st until piece measures 6.5 (6.5, 6.25, 5.75, 5.75) (6, 6, 6.5, 6.75)" [16.5 (16.5, 16, 14.5, 14.5) (15, 15, 16.5, 17) cm].

BEG CHART

Work Rnds 1–58 of Sweater Chart.

DIVIDE FOR FRONT/BACK

Division Rnd: Working Rnd 59 of chart, work 10 (12, 14, 16, 18) (22, 26, 30, 32) sts. Place on st holder for underarm, work 86 (96, 106, 116, 126) (134, 142, 150, 160) sts for front, work 10 (12, 14, 16, 18) (22, 26, 30, 32) sts and place on st holder for underarm, work to end of back—86 (96, 106, 116, 126) (134, 142, 150, 160) sts rem each for front and back.

YOKE

Note: Continue to work patterns as established within each section until chart is complete, then work in F for remainder. Raglan columns will consist of 4 sts in F; these columns will separate back/front charts from sleeve charts.

— *Joining Rnd:* With yarn attached to back and continuing chart pattern as established, k2 with F, work across left sleeve to last 2 sleeve sts, k2 with F, pm, k2 with F, work across front to last 2 front sts, k2 with F, pm, k2 with F, work across right sleeve to last 2 sts, k2 with F, pm, k2 with F, work across back to last 2 back sts, k2 with F; pm for beg of rnd—302 (322, 350, 390, 426) (442, 458, 474, 502) sts.

SHAPE YOKE AND NECK

Note: Body and sleeve instructions are given separately but worked at same time. Body shaping is worked between front and back markers; sleeve shaping is worked between sleeve markers. Front neck shaping beg before yoke shaping is complete; once front neck shaping begins, piece is worked back and forth in rows. Work yoke shaping as follows:

— *On Dec Rnds/RS Dec Rows:* (With F, k1, ssk), work in pattern to 3 sts before marker, (with F, k2tog, k1)— 2 sts dec in each shaped section.

— *On WS Dec Rows:* (With F, p1, ssp), work in pattern to 3 sts before marker, (with F, p2tog, p1)—2 sts dec in each shaped section.

— Body Shaping: Working Dec Rnds/ Rows as given above, dec 2 sts each for front and back on 1st yoke rnd, then every other rnd/row 16 (25, 30, 28, 25) (23, 23, 20, 17) times, then every 4 (4, 1, 1, 1) (1, 1, 1, 1) rnd(s)/row(s) 6 (2, 2, 8, 16) (20, 24, 30, 38) times.

— Sleeve Shaping: Working Dec Rnds/ Rows as given above, dec 2 sts each sleeve on first yoke rnd, then every

other rnd/row 24 (21, 23, 28, 32) (32, 33, 33, 36) more times, then every 4 (4, 4, 4, 1) (1, 4, 4, 0) rnd(s)/row(s) 2 (4, 4, 2, 2) (2, 1, 1, 0) time(s).

— AT THE SAME TIME, when armholes measure 6.5 (6.75, 7.5, 7.5, 7.75) (7.75, 8.25, 8.25, 8.5)" [16.5 (17, 19, 19, 19.5) (19.5, 21, 21, 21.5) cm], work front neck shaping as follows:

— Place removable marker either side of 12 (12, 12, 12, 12) (14, 14, 14, 14) center front sts.

Note: Continue to work yoke shaping as established for remainder of piece.

— Neck Shaping: Next Rnd: Work to second neck marker, place neck sts between markers on st holder, work to end. Cut yarn and slide left sleeve and left front sts to right needle.

— Rejoin yarn at right front. Working back and forth in rows, BO 5 (6, 6, 6, 6) (7, 7, 7, 7) sts at beg of next 2 rows, 3 (3, 3, 3, 3) (3, 3, 4, 4) sts at beg of next 4 rows, then dec 1 st at each neck edge every RS row 1 (0, 0, 1, 1) (1, 1, 0, 0) time(s), as follows: K1, ssk, work to last 3 sts, k2tog, k1.

— Continue until all shaping is complete, ending with a WS row—66 (70, 70, 80, 80) (84, 84, 86, 86) sts rem; 40 (40, 40, 42, 42) (46, 46, 48, 48) sts for back, 2 sts each front, and 11 (13, 13, 17, 17) (17, 17, 17, 17) sts each sleeve. Cut yarn.

NECKBAND

— *Next Row (RS):* Slide right front
and right sleeve sts to right needle.
Rejoin yarn and pm for beg of rnd.
With smaller circular needle, knit
to end of left front, pick up and knit
15 (15, 15, 16, 16) (17, 17, 18, 18) sts
to held center front sts, knit across
held sts, pick up and knit 15 (15, 15,
16, 16) (17, 17, 18, 18) sts along right
front neck edge, knit to beg-of-rnd
marker—108 (112, 112, 124, 124)
(132, 132, 136, 136) sts.

— Beg 2×2 Rib; work even for 1.25"
(3 cm). BO all sts in pattern.

FINISHING

With RS facing, join underarm sts using
grafting (see right) or using 3-Needle BO,
as follows:

— Place underarm sts on 2 spare
needles. Hold sides with RSs facing
each other, needles parallel. Using
3rd needle, always working 1st st
on front needle tog with first st on
back needle, k2tog, *k2tog, pass first
st over second st to BO first st; rep
from * until all underarm sts are BO.

— Weave in ends; block as desired.

GRAFTING STITCHES

— Using a blunt tapestry needle, thread a length of yarn approximately 4 times the length of the section to be joined.

— With stitches still on the needles, hold the pieces to be joined parallel, with WSs together, both needle tips pointing to the right. Working from right to left:

Setup

— Insert tapestry needle into first stitch on front needle purlwise, pull yarn through, leaving stitch on needle.

— Insert tapestry needle into first stitch on back needle knitwise, pull yarn through, leaving stitch on needle.

Repeat for all stitches

— *Insert tapestry needle into first stitch on front needle knitwise, pull yarn through, remove stitch from needle.

— Insert tapestry needle into next stitch on front needle purlwise, pull yarn through, leave stitch on needle.

— Insert tapestry needle into first stitch on back needle purlwise, pull yarn through, remove stitch from needle.

— Insert tapestry needle into next stitch on back needle knitwise, pull yarn through, leave stitch on needle.

— Repeat from *, adjusting stitch tension every 3 or 4 stitches to match the pieces being joined.

— When 1 stitch remains on each needle, cut yarn and pass through last 2 stitches to fasten off.

COFFEE
BREAK

ARNE AND CARLOS really know how to make the most of a day, and *fika* is one of their favorite rituals. When they talk about *fika*, all we want is to get our *fika* going too.

What's *fika*? It's coffee and cake with a friend, a Swedish tradition that Arne and Carlos embrace wholeheartedly. Many Norwegians call it *kaffepause*. Whatever! We call it brilliant.

There is an impressive devotion to *fika* and *kaffepause*. Companies schedule a *kaffepause* into their standard work day. Schools do too. How nice is that?

And there's cake. Or a cinnamon bun. Or whatever delicious baked good is at hand.

And, most important, *fika* is meant to include a bit of time with a friend or a co-worker. It's a moment to share together. A pause for a bit of coziness.

This simple ritual sounds exactly like our cup of . . . *kaffe*.

ROSY MITTENS

Design by
Arne & Carlos

A T FIRST SIGHT, the Rosy Mittens sent Kay flying back to a rapture-filled story in *Little House in the Big Woods*, in which Mary and Laura Ingalls's Christmas presents included mittens made by their mother Caroline. As a child of the plains, who grew up with deathly cold winters that lasted until May, Kay understands that a gift of mittens means someone loves you—and wants you to survive.

This pair from Arne and Carlos is practical and beautiful, just as good Norwegian mittens should be. Knit to a firm gauge for warmth and durability, they feature folkloric swirls on the top of the hand and thumb and checker-like diamonds on the bottom. They can be worked in the five colors shown at left all at once; they can be worked in just the two main colors (here red and white) with the extra color flourishes added with duplicate stitch; or they can be worked in two colors only (for example, see the red and black mitten on page 31). Make your choice and make a pair for someone you want to keep warm, inside and out.

KNITTED MEASUREMENTS

Hand Circumference: 9.75 (10.25)" [25 (26) cm]

Length: 12.5 (13.25)" [32 (33.5) cm]

SIZE

To fit adult medium (large)

MATERIALS

— Norwegian Wool by Arne & Carlos for Rowan [50 g skeins, each approx 137 yds (125 m), 100% wool]: 1 ball each A, B, C, D, and E
Colorway 1: #018 Ribbon Red (A), #014 Cloud Dancer (B), #012 Gold Nugget (C), #020 Frost Pink (D), and #011 Daphne (E)
Colorway 2: #018 Ribbon Red (A), #019 Peat (B), #012 Gold Nugget (C), #020 Frost Pink (D), and #011 Daphne (E)

— Size US 1 (2.25 mm) double-pointed needles (set of 4 or 5)

— Size US 3 (3.25 mm) double-pointed needles (set of 4 or 5), or size needed to achieve gauge

— Stitch marker

— Waste yarn

GAUGE

24 sts and 28 rnds = 4" (10 cm) over stranded st st, using larger needles, blocked

STITCH PATTERN

Half Twisted Rib (even number of sts)

All Rnds: *K1-tbl, p1; rep from * to end.

Duplicate Stitch (optional): Using a tapestry needle, and beginning at the right end of the row to be worked, *bring the yarn up from the WS through the bottom center of the first stitch to be duplicated. Thread the needle from right to left under both legs of the stitch immediately above the current st, then insert the needle back down into the center of the current stitch to the WS and bring it out through the bottom center of the next stitch to the left; repeat from * until the entire row is complete, ending with the yarn to the WS.

NOTE

If you prefer to work using only two colors per rnd, you may work all sts shown in C, D, and E using B instead, then once the mittens are complete, you may work the sts in C, D, and E using duplicate st. For the two-color sample, C, D, and E were omitted.

LEFT MITTEN

CUFF

— Using smaller needles and A, CO 46 (50) sts. Join, being careful not to twist sts; pm for beg of rnd and work as follows:

— Beg Half Twisted Rib; work 30 rnds, changing colors as follows: 2 rnds A, 5 rnds B, 2 rnds A, 3 rnds B, 2 rnds A, 1 rnd B, then 15 rnds A.

HAND

— Change to larger needles.
— Knit 1 rnd.

SHAPE THUMB GUSSET

— Beg Left Hand Chart for your size; work Rnds 1–15 (17)—58 (62) sts after Rnd 15 (17).

— *Next Rnd:* Work Rnd 16 (18) of chart to last 14 sts, change to waste yarn, k13 and slide these 13 sts back to left needle, drop waste yarn and change back to working yarn; continue working chart to end.

WORK HAND AND SHAPE TOP

— Continue until chart is complete, working decs as indicated in chart—10 sts rem after Rnd 61 (66).

— Cut yarn, leaving long tail. Thread tail through rem sts, pull tight, and fasten off.

THUMB

Carefully remove waste yarn from thumb sts and place 13 bottom and 13 top sts onto larger needles. Rejoin working yarn at bottom right edge of thumb opening. Join; pm for beg of rnd and work as follows:

— Beg Thumb Chart for your size; work Rnds 1–22 (26), working incs and decs as indicated in chart—28 sts after Rnd 1; 8 sts rem after Rnd 22 (26).

— Cut yarn, leaving long tail. Thread tail through rem sts, pull tight, and fasten off.

RIGHT MITTEN

Work as for left mitten to beg of hand.

HAND

Change to larger needles.

SHAPE THUMB GUSSET

— Beg Right Hand Chart for your size; work Rnds 1–15 (17)—58 (62) sts after Rnd 15 (17).

— *Next Rnd:* Work Rnd 16 (18) of chart over 30 (32) sts, change to waste yarn, k13 and slide these 13 sts back to left needle, drop waste yarn and change back to working yarn; continue working chart to end.

WORK HAND AND SHAPE TOP

— Continue until chart is complete, working decs as indicated in chart—10 sts rem after Rnd 61 (66).

— Cut yarn, leaving long tail. Thread tail through rem sts, pull tight, and fasten off.

THUMB

Work as for left mitten.

FINISHING

Weave in ends. Block as desired.

Left Hand Chart: Size Medium

Left Hand Chart – Size Medium

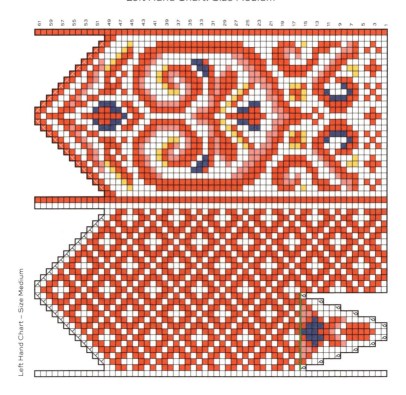

Thumb Chart – Size Medium

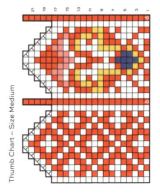

Right Hand Chart: Size Medium

Right Hand Chart – Size Medium

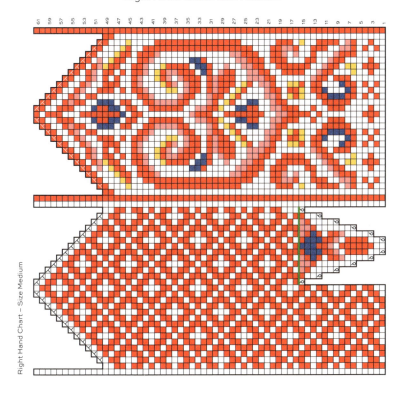

Stitch Key

☐ Knit
⧄ M1L
⧅ M1R
⊠ K2tog
⊠ Ssk
▮ Waste yarn

Color Key

🟥 A
⬜ B
🟨 C
🟪 D
🟦 E

Left Hand Chart: Size Large

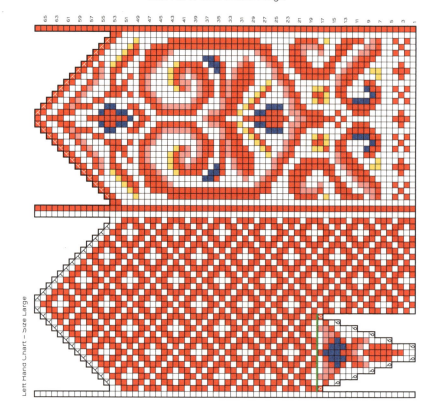

Left Hand Chart – Size Large

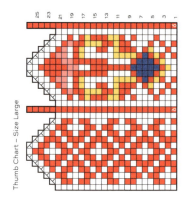

Thumb Chart – Size Large

Right Hand Chart: Size Large

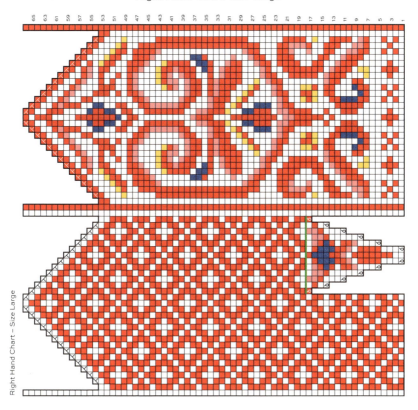

Right Hand Chart – Size Large

Stitch Key

Knit · M1L · M1R · K2tog · Ssk · Waste yarn

Color Key

A · B · C · D · E

KOS NECKWARMER

Design by
Arne & Carlos

CENTURIES OF HARD, dark winters have made *kos*—a Norwegian word evoking warmth, light, and closeness—an essential part of the culture. The Kos Neckwarmer is a handy, happy-making piece for anyone who braves the cold. It's worked from the bottom up, following a simple colorwork chart that marks out the yoke decreases, and finishes with a ribbed fold-over collar. If you're feeling tempted to make the Valdres Pullover but are not ready to commit, try this whimsical accessory as a warmup (in every sense of the word).

KNITTED MEASUREMENTS

Approx 49.5" (125.5 cm) circumference
along lower edge x 13.25" (33.5 cm) length

MATERIALS

— Norwegian Wool by Arne & Carlos
  for Rowan [50 g skeins, each approx
  137 yds (125 m), 100% wool]: 2 balls
  #019 Peat (B); 1 ball each #018
  Ribbon Red (A), #014 Cloud Dancer
  (C), and #017 Emerald (D)
— Size US 2 (3 mm) circular needle,
  24" (60 cm) long
— Size US 4 (3.5 mm) circular needle,
  16" and 24" (40 and 60 cm) long, or
  size needed to achieve gauge
— Stitch marker

GAUGE

22 sts and 28 rnds = 4" (10 cm) over
stranded st st, using larger needle,
blocked

STITCH PATTERN

2×2 Rib (multiple of 4 sts)
All Rnds: *K2, p2; rep from * to end.

Neckwarmer Chart

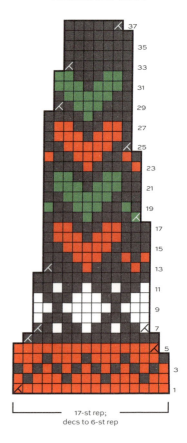

17-st rep;
decs to 6-st rep

Stitch Key

☐ Knit

◩ K2tog

Color Key

■ A

■ B

☐ C

■ D

NECKWARMER

- Using smaller needle and A, CO 272 sts. Join, being careful not to twist sts; pm for beg of rnd and work in the rnd as follows:
- Beg 2×2 Rib; work 4 rnds even.
- Change to D; work 5 rnds even.
- Change to larger needle.
- Beg Neckwarmer Chart; work Rnds 1–37 of chart, working decs as indicated in chart—96 sts rem after Rnd 37. Cut A, C, and D; continue with B for remainder of piece.
- Change to smaller needle.
- Beg 2×2 Rib; work 6.75" (17 cm) even.
- BO loosely in pattern.

FINISHING
Weave in ends. Block as desired.

ABBREVIATIONS

Approx: Approximately
Beg: Begin(ning)(s)
BO: Bind off
CO: Cast on
Dec: Decreas(ed)(es)(ing)
Dpn: Double-pointed needle(s)
Inc: Increas(ed)(es)(ing)
K: Knit
K2tog: Knit 2 stitches together. One stitch has been decreased.
M1L: (Make 1 left) Insert left needle from front to back under horizontal strand between stitch just worked and the next stitch on the left needle. Knit this strand through the back loop. One stitch has been increased.
M1R: (Make 1 right) Insert left needle from back to front under horizontal strand between stitch just worked and the next stitch on the left needle. Knit this strand through the front loop. One stitch has been increased.
P: Purl
P2tog: Purl 2 stitches together. One stitch has been decreased.

Pm: Place marker
Rep: Repeat(ed)(ing)(s)
Rnd(s): Round(s)
RS: Right side
Ssk: Slip 1 stitch knitwise, slip 1 stitch purlwise, insert left needle into front of these 2 stitches; knit together from this position. 1 stitch dec'd.

Ssp:	Slip 2 stitches 1 at a time knitwise, slip them back to the left needle in their new orientation, purl them together through the back loops. One stitch has been decreased.	**Tbl:**	Through the back loop(s)
		Tog:	Together
		WS:	Wrong side
St st:	Stockinette stitch		
St(s):	Stitch(es)		

Build your collection of MDK Field Guides.
Choose any three or more and save 15%.
Visit **www.ModernDailyKnitting.com**.